HAL•LEONARD BASS PLAY-ALONG

LENNON AND McCARTNEY

VOL. 13

Tracking, mixing, and mastering by
Jake Johnson & Bill Maynard at Paradyme Productions
Bass by Tom McGirr
Guitars by Doug Boduch
Keyboards by Warren Wiegratz
Drums by Scott Schroedl

ISBN 978-1-4234-1421-6

HAL•LEONARD® CORPORATION
7777 W. Bluemound Rd. P.O. Box 13819 Milwaukee, WI 53213

Visit Hal Leonard Online at
www.halleonard.com

Bass Notation Legend

Bass music can be notated two different ways: on a *musical staff*, and in *tablature*

THE MUSICAL STAFF shows pitches and rhythms and is divided by bar lines into measures. Pitches are named after the first seven letters of the alphabet.

TABLATURE graphically represents the bass fingerboard. Each horizontal line represents a string, and each number represents a fret.

3rd string, open   2nd string, 2nd fret   1st & 2nd strings open, played together

HAMMER-ON: Strike the first (lower) note with one finger, then sound the higher note (on the same string) with another finger by fretting it without picking.

PULL-OFF: Place both fingers on the notes to be sounded. Strike the first note and without picking, pull the finger off to sound the second (lower) note.

LEGATO SLIDE: Strike the first note and then slide the same fret-hand finger up or down to the second note. The second note is not struck.

SHIFT SLIDE: Same as legato slide, except the second note is struck.

TRILL: Very rapidly alternate between the notes indicated by continuously hammering on and pulling off.

TREMOLO PICKING: The note is picked as rapidly and continuously as possible.

VIBRATO: The string is vibrated by rapidly bending and releasing the note with the fretting hand.

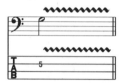

SHAKE: Using one finger, rapidly alternate between two notes on one string by sliding either a half-step above or below.

NATURAL HARMONIC: Strike the note while the fret hand lightly touches the string directly over the fret indicated.

MUFFLED STRINGS: A percussive sound is produced by laying the fret hand across the string(s) without depressing them and striking them with the pick hand.

BEND: Strike the note and bend up the interval shown.

BEND AND RELEASE: Strike the note and bend up as indicated, then release back to the original note. Only the first note is struck.

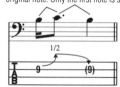

RIGHT-HAND TAP: Hammer ("tap") the fret indicated with the "pick-hand" index or middle finger and pull off to the note fretted by the fret hand.

LEFT-HAND TAP: Hammer ("tap") the fret indicated with the "fret-hand" index or middle finger.

SLAP: Strike ("slap") string with right-hand thumb.

POP: Snap ("pop") string with right-hand index or middle finger.

Additional Musical Definitions

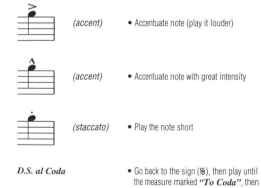

(accent)   • Accentuate note (play it louder)

(accent)   • Accentuate note with great intensity

(staccato)   • Play the note short

D.S. al Coda   • Go back to the sign (𝄋), then play until the measure marked *"To Coda"*, then skip to the section labelled *"Coda."*

Fill   • Label used to identify a brief pattern which is to be inserted into the arrangement.

• Repeat measures between signs.

• When a repeated section has different endings, play the first ending only the first time and the second ending only the second time.

CONTENTS

All My Loving

Words and Music by John Lennon and Paul McCartney

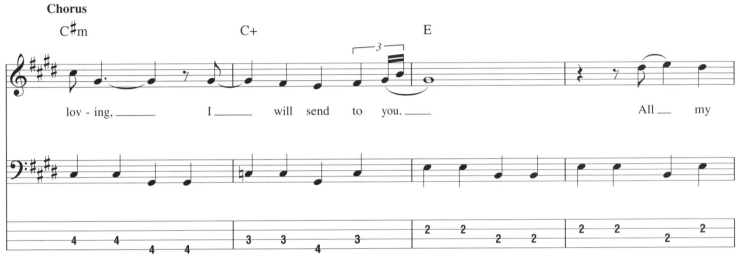

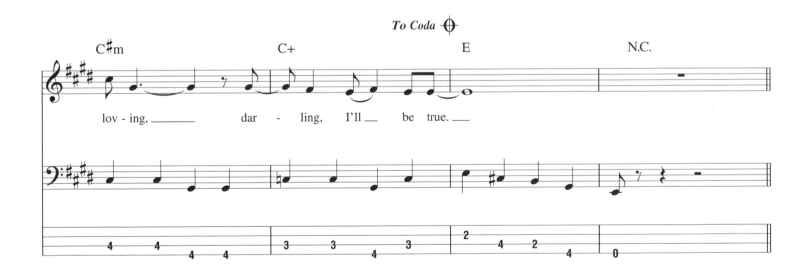

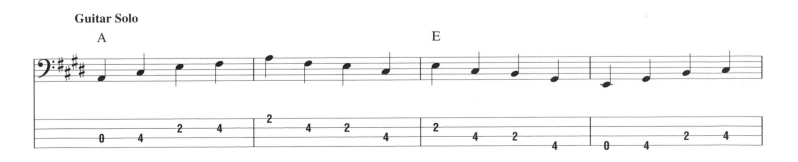

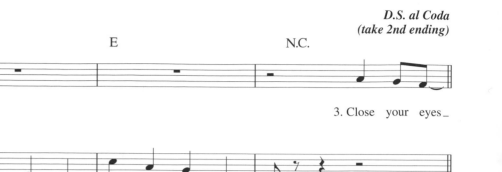

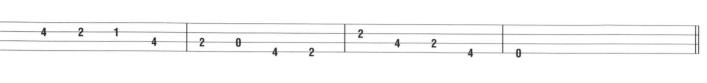

 Coda

Additional Lyrics

2. I'll pretend that I'm kissing
   The lips I am missing,
   And hope that my dreams will come true.
   And then while I'm away,
   I'll write home ev'ry day,
   And I'll send all my loving to you.

Day Tripper

Words and Music by John Lennon and Paul McCartney

Intro
Moderate Rock ♩ = 138

Chorus

day _____ trip-per; one way tick - et, yeah. __ It took me

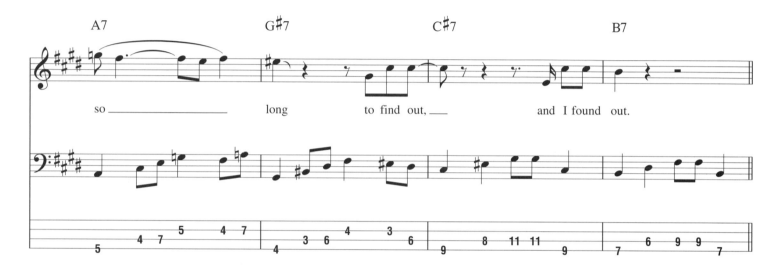

so _____ long to find out, ___ and I found out.

Interlude

D.S. al Coda 1

⊕ **Coda 1**

Chorus

day _____ trip - per;

one way tick - et, yeah. ___ It took me so ___

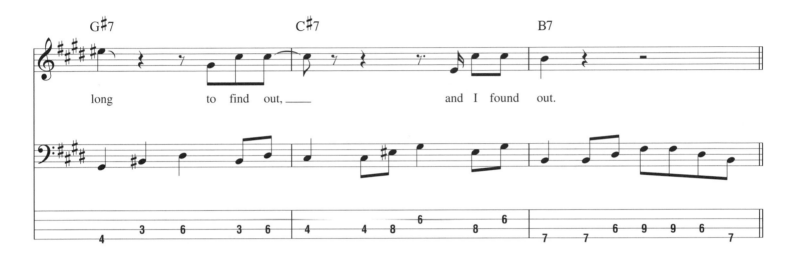

long to find out, ___ and I found out.

Interlude

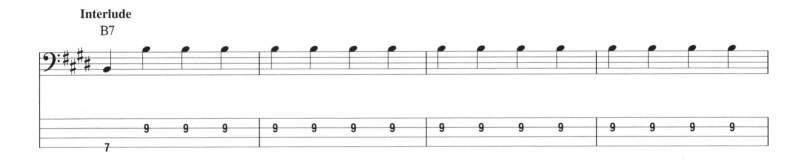

Guitar Solo

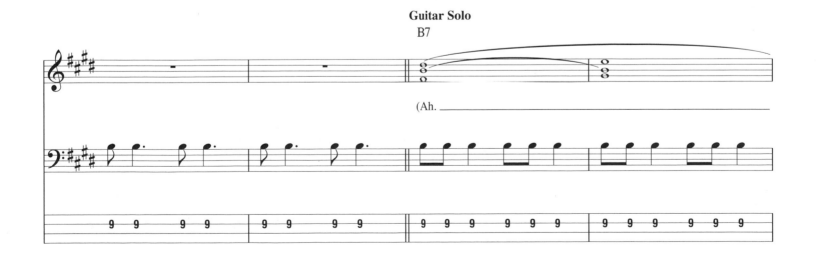

(Ah. ___

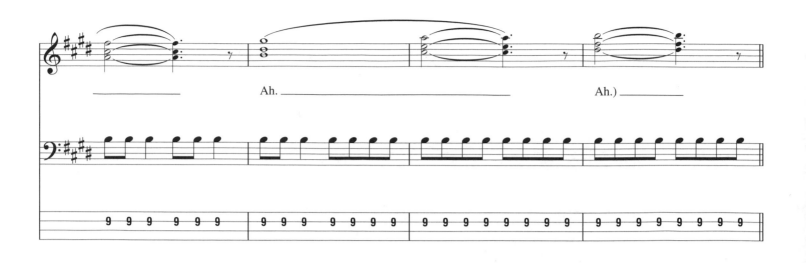

Ah. _____ Ah.) _____

Breakdown

E7

D.S. al Coda 2

⊕ **Coda 2**

so _____ long to find out, ___ and I found out.

Breakdown

E7

Play 3 times

Outro

E7

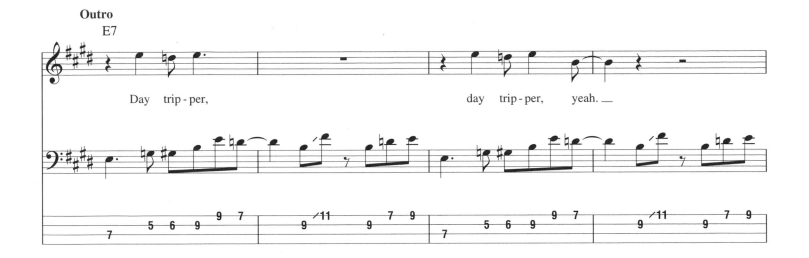

Day trip - per, day trip - per, yeah. __

Begin fade

Day trip - per, day trip - per, yeah. __

Fade out

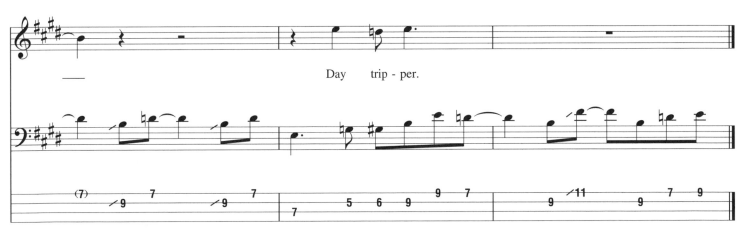

__ Day trip - per.

Additional Lyrics

2. She's a big teaser.
She took me half the way there.
She's a big teaser.
She took me half the way there, now.

3. Tried to please her.
She only played one night stands.
Tried to please her.
She only played one night stands, now.

Back in the U.S.S.R.

Words and Music by John Lennon and Paul McCartney

Intro
Driving Rock ♩ = 144

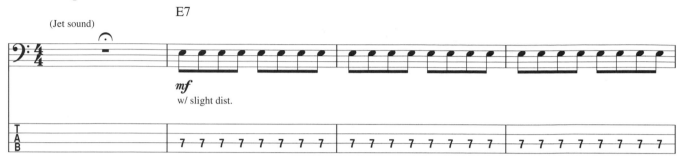

(Jet sound)

E7

mf
w/ slight dist.

Verse

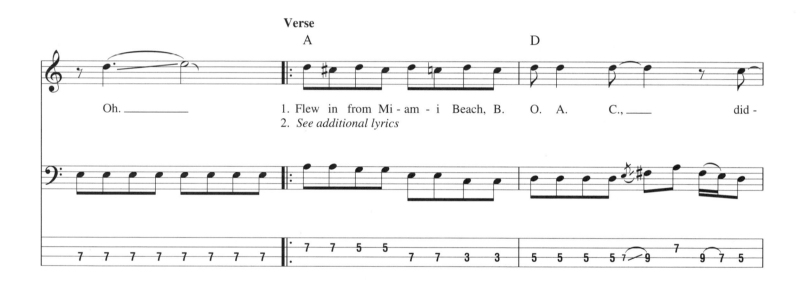

A   D

Oh. _____

1. Flew in from Mi - am - i Beach, B.   O.   A.   C., _____ did -
2. *See additional lyrics*

C   D   A

- n't get to bed last   night. ___   On ___ the way the pa - per bag was

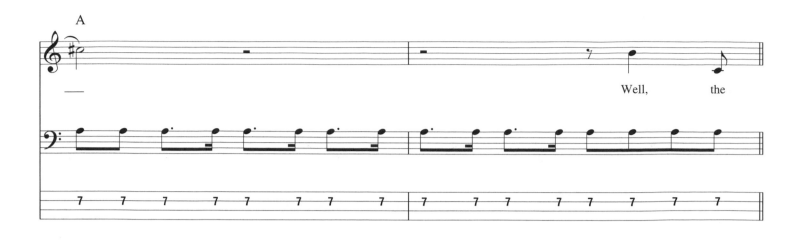

A

Well, the

Bridge

D   **A**

U - kraine girls real - ly knock me out, __ they leave the __ west be - hind. __

D   **D♭**   **C**   **B**

And Mos - cow girls make me sing and shout, __ that

To Coda

E7   **D7**   **A**   **B** **E7**

Geor-gia's al - ways on my mi-mi - mi-mi-mi-mi-mi-mi __ mind. __   Oh, come on!

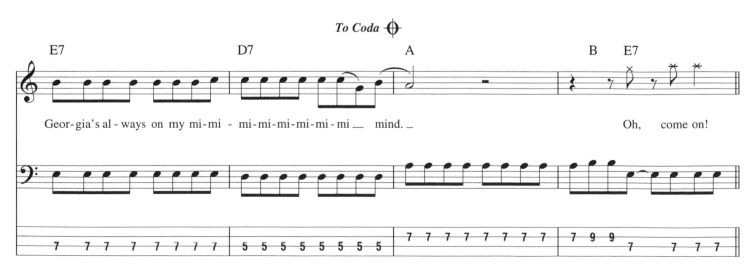

Verse

— me 'round your snow peaked moun-tains way down south, — take — me to your dad-dy's farm. —

— Let — me hear your bal - a - lai - kas ring-ing out. — Come —

— and keep your com - rade — warm. I'm back in the U. S. S. R. —

Chorus

— Hey! You don't — know how luck - y you are, — boys. —

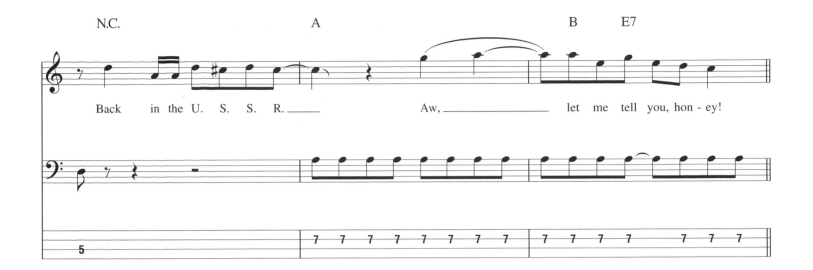

Back in the U. S. S. R. ___ Aw, _____ let me tell you, hon - ey!

Outro

A

Hey, I'm _ back!

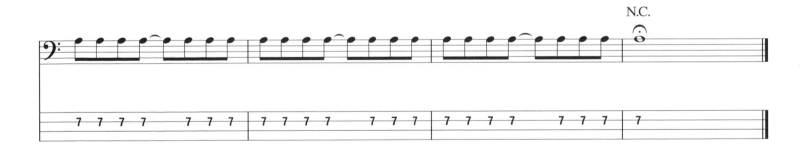

Additional Lyrics

2. Been away so long I hardly knew the place.
   Gee, it's good to get back home.
   Leave it till tomorrow to unpack my case.
   Honey, disconnect the phone.
   I'm back in the U.S.S.R.,...

Eight Days a Week

Words and Music by John Lennon and Paul McCartney

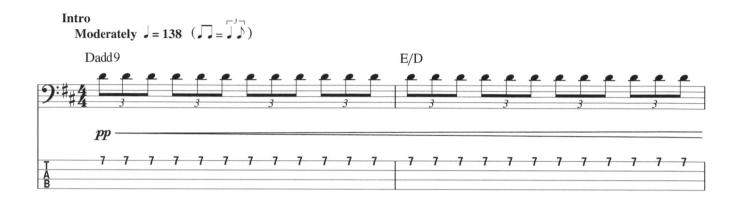

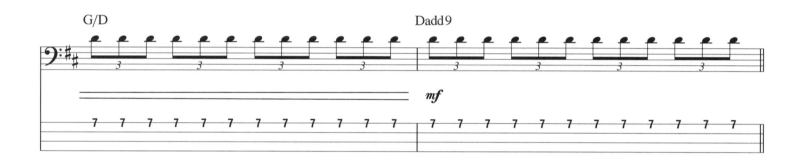

1., 3. Oo, I need your love, babe, _ guess you know it's true. ___
2., 4. *See additional lyrics*

Additional Lyrics

2., 4. Love you ev'ry day, girl,
Always on my mind.
One thing I can say, girl,
Love you all the time.

Get Back

Words and Music by John Lennon and Paul McCartney

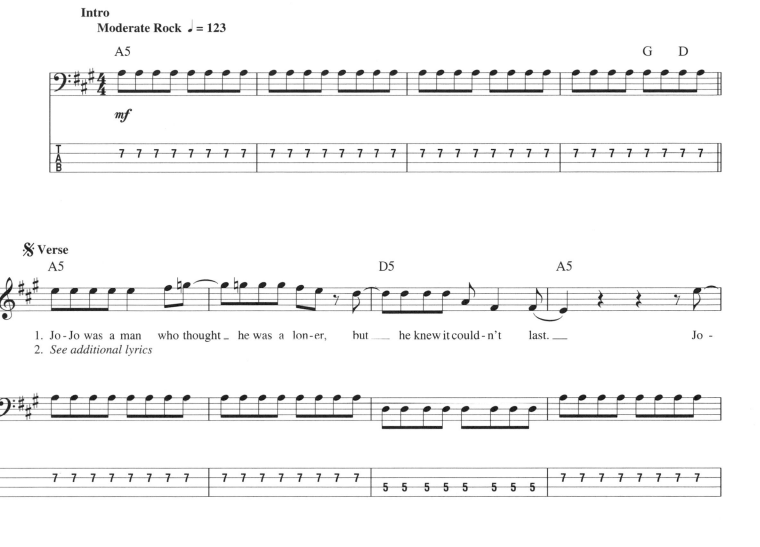

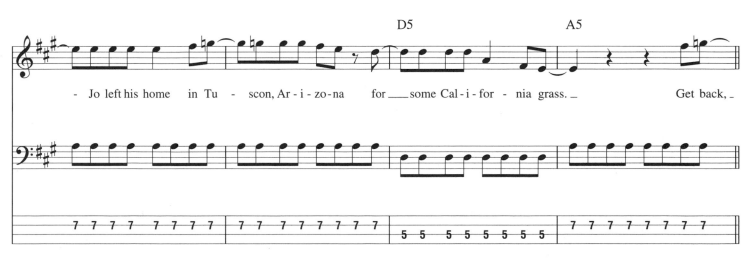

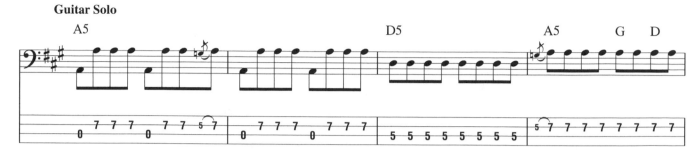

⊕ Coda

Guitar Solo

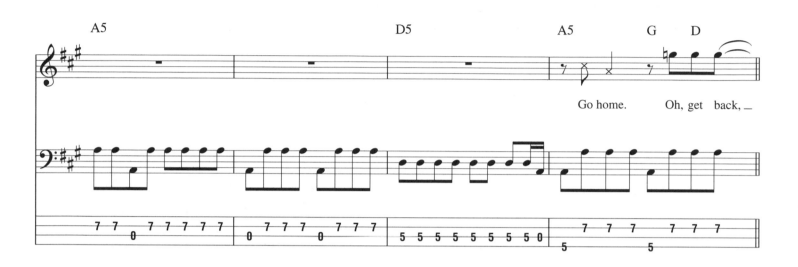

Go home. Oh, get back, _

Chorus

_ you get back, _ get back _ to where you once be - longed. _ Ya, get back, _

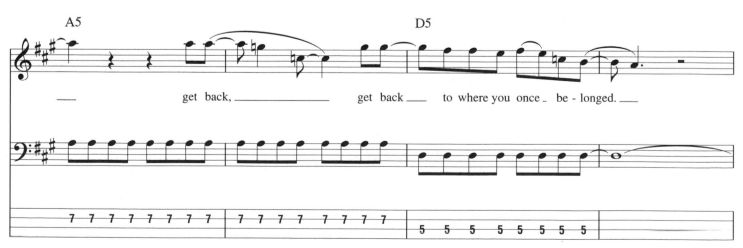

_ get back, _ get back _ to where you once _ be - longed. _

Outro

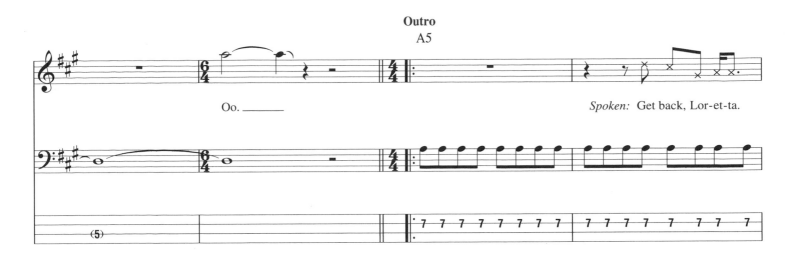

Oo. _____

Spoken: Get back, Lor-et-ta.

2nd time, Begin fade

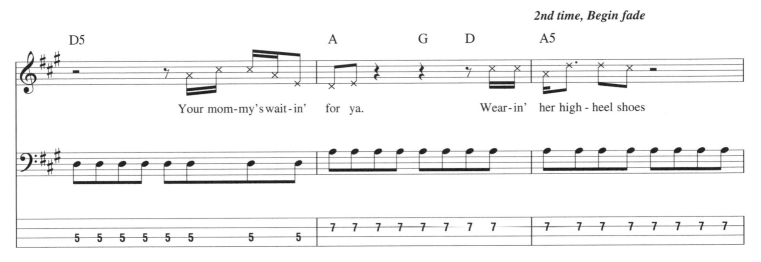

Your mom-my's wait-in' for ya.

Wear-in' her high - heel shoes

2nd time, Fade out

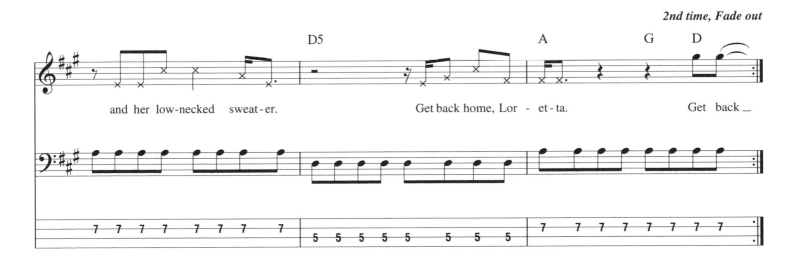

and her low-necked sweat-er.

Get back home, Lor - et-ta.

Get back _____

Additional Lyrics

2. Sweet Loretta Martin thought she was a woman,
   But she was another man.
   All the girls around her say she's got it coming,
   But she gets it while she can.

I Saw Her Standing There

Words and Music by John Lennon and Paul McCartney

2nd time, substitute Fill 1

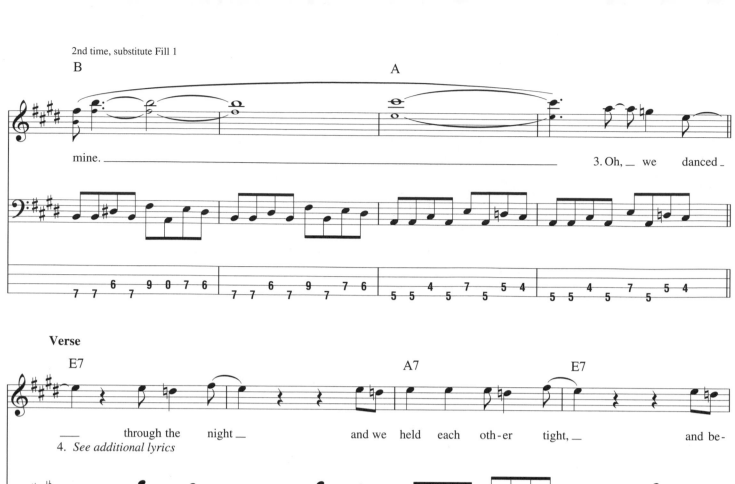

mine. _____ 3. Oh, __ we danced __

Verse

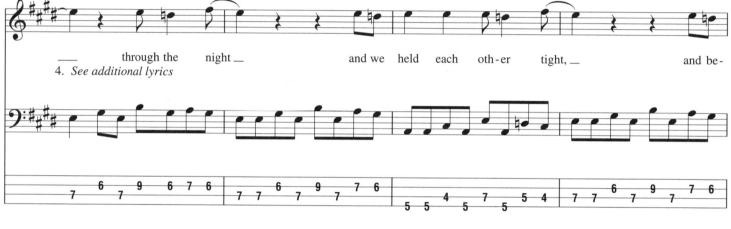

___ through the night __ and we held each oth-er tight, __ and be-
4. *See additional lyrics*

To Coda ⊕

fore too long __ I fell in love __ with her. _____ Now,

Fill 1

28

I'll nev-er dance __ with an-oth-er, oh, ____ since I

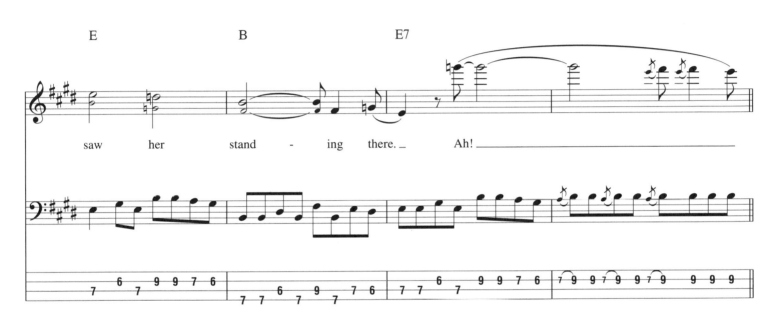

saw her stand-ing there. __ Ah! ____

Guitar Solo

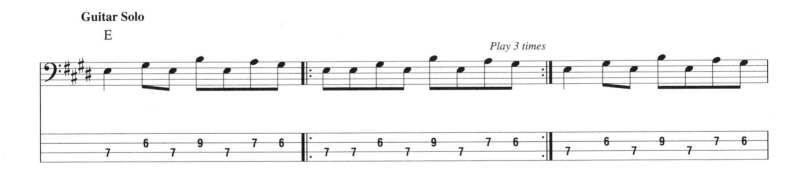

Play 3 times

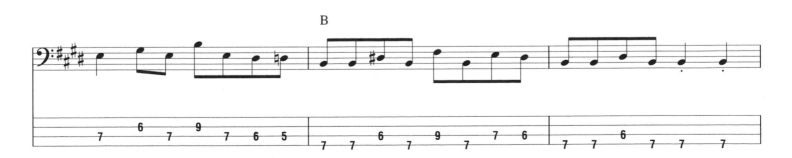

D.S. al Coda

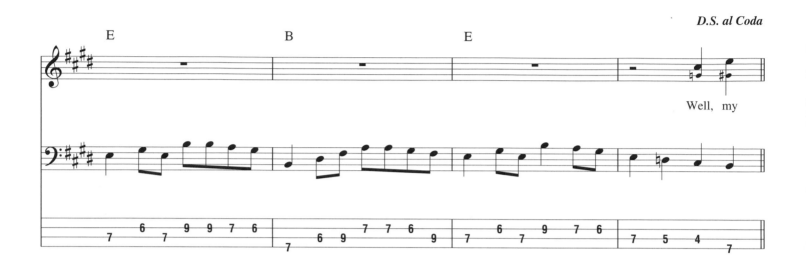

Well, my

Coda

Now   I'll   nev - er   dance ___   with an - oth -

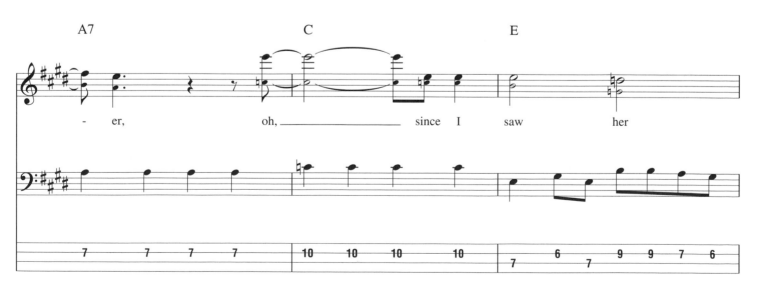

- er,   oh, _____ since I   saw   her

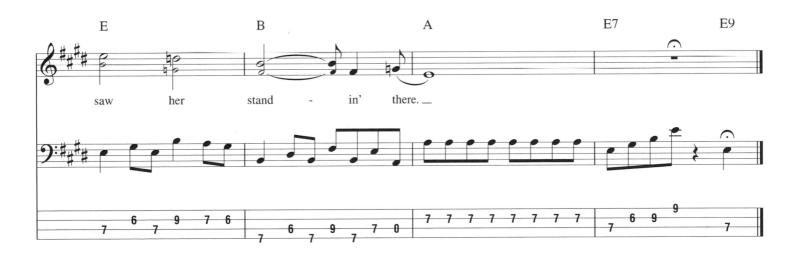

Additional Lyrics

2. Well, she looked at me
   And I, I could see
   That before too long I'd fall in love with her.
   She wouldn't dance with another, ooh,
   When I saw her standing there.

4. Oh, we danced through the night
   And we held each other tight,
   And before too long I fell in love with her.
   Now I'll never dance with another, ooh,
   Since I saw her standin' there.

Paperback Writer

Words and Music by John Lennon and Paul McCartney

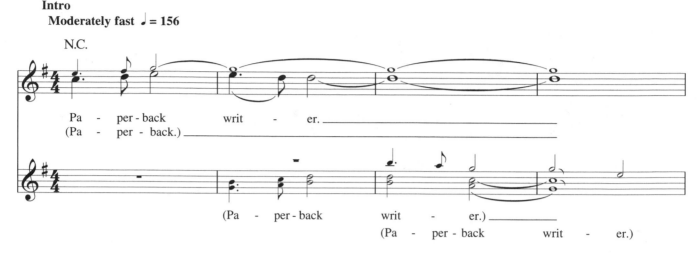

based on a nov-el by a man named Lear. And I need a job, __ so I want to be a pa-per-back

To Coda ⊕

C   G7

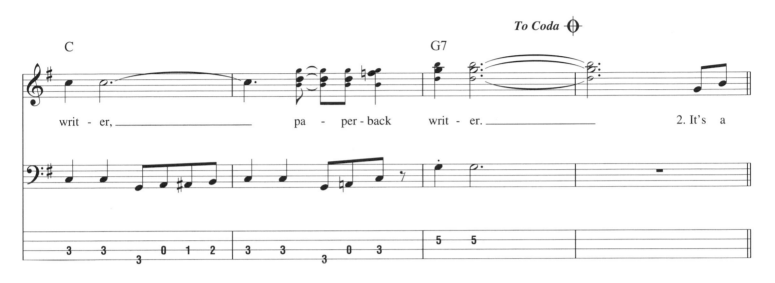

writ - er, _____ pa - per - back writ - er. _____ 2. It's a

Verse

G7

dirt - y sto - ry of a dirt - y man, _ and his cling-ing wife _ does-n't un-der-stand. His

son is work - ing for the Dai - ly Mail, _ it's a stead - y job _ but he wants to be a pa-per-back

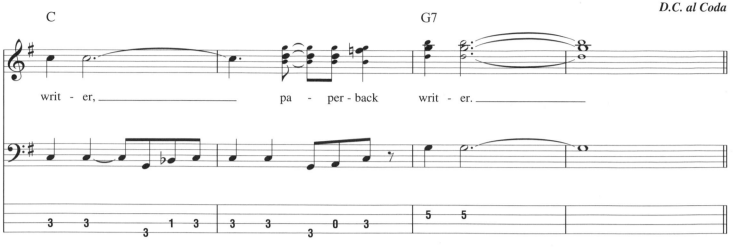

writ - er, _____ pa - per - back writ - er. _____

Coda

Verse

4. If you real - ly like __ it you can have the rights, _ it could

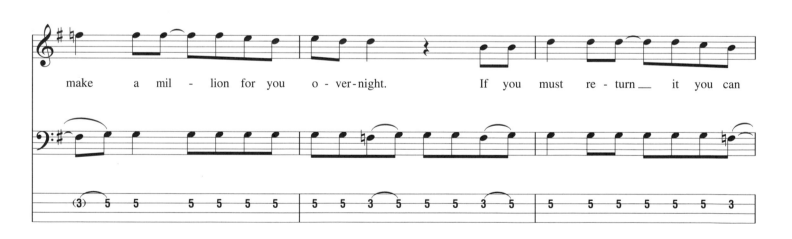

make a mil - lion for you o - ver-night. If you must re - turn __ it you can

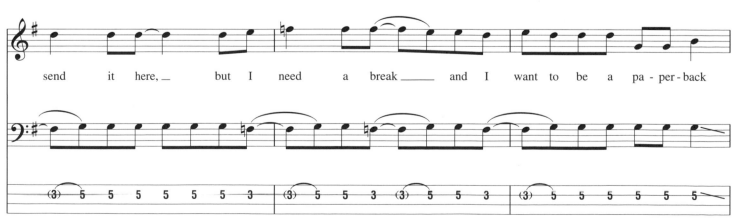

send it here, __ but I need a break _____ and I want to be a pa - per - back

Additional Lyrics

3. It's a thousand pages, give or take a few;
   I'll be writing more in a week or two.
   I can make it longer if you like the style.
   I can change it 'round,
   And I want to be a paperback writer,
   Paperback writer.

Nowhere Man

Words and Music by John Lennon and Paul McCartney

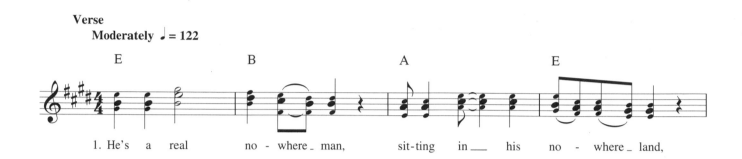

Verse

Moderately ♩ = 122

1. He's a real no - where _ man, sit-ting in _ his no - where _ land,

mak-ing all _ his no - where plans for no - bod-y.

Verse

2. Does-n't have _ a point of view, _ knows not where he's go-ing to. _

Is-n't he ___ a bit ___ like you ___ and me? _____ No - where man, ___

𝄋 Chorus

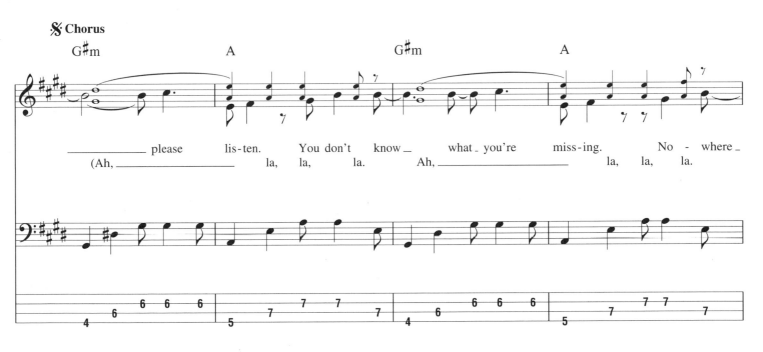

_____ please lis-ten. You don't know ___ what you're miss-ing. No - where ___
(Ah, _____ la, la, la. Ah, _____ la, la, la.

To Coda ⊕

___ man, ___ the world _____ is at your com-mand.
Ah, _____ la, la, la. Ah, _____ la, la, la, la.)

Guitar Solo

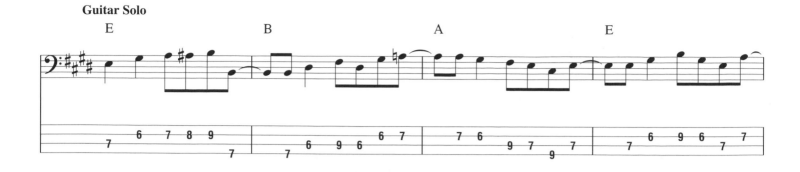

Verse

3. He's as blind as he can be, ___ just sees what he wants to see. ___

No-where man, _ can you see me at all? ___ No-where man, _